A W
AND OTHER POEMS

BY
GEORGE STERLING
AUTHOR OF "TESTIMONY OF THE
SUNS"

FIRST PUBLISHED: 1909
THIS EDITION: 2016

CONTENTS

A WINE OF WIZARDRY

"When mountains were stained as with wine
By the dawning of Time, and as wine
Were the seas."   AMBROSE BIERCE.

Without, the battlements of sunset shine,
'Mid domes the sea-winds rear and overwhelm.
Into a crystal cup the dusky wine
I pour, and, musing at so rich a shrine,
I watch the star that haunts its ruddy gloom.
Now Fancy, empress of a purpled realm,
Awakes with brow caressed by poppy-bloom,
And wings in sudden dalliance her flight
To strands where opals of the shattered light
Gleam in the wind-strewn foam, and maidens flee
A little past the striving billows' reach,
Or seek the russet mosses of the sea,
And wrinkled shells that lure along the beach,
And please the heart of Fancy; yet she turns,
Tho' trembling, to a grotto rosy-sparred,
Where wattled monsters redly gape, that guard
A cowled magician peering on the damned
Thro' vials wherein a splendid poison burns,
Sifting Satanic gules athwart his brow.
So Fancy will not gaze with him, and now
She wanders to an iceberg oriflammed
With rayed, auroral guidons of the North—
Wherein hath winter hidden ardent gems
And treasuries of frozen anadems,

Alight with timid sapphires of the snow.
But she would dream of warmer gems, and so
Ere long her eyes in fastnesses look forth
O'er blue profounds mysterious whence glow
The coals of Tartarus on the moonless air,
As Titans plan to storm Olympus' throne,
'Mid pulse of dungeoned forges down the stunned,
Undominated firmament, and glare
Of Cyclopean furnaces unsunned.

Then hastens she in refuge to a lone,
Immortal garden of the eastern hours,
Where Dawn upon a pansy's breast hath laid
A single tear, and whence the wind hath flown
And left a silence. Far on the shadowy tow'rs
Droop blazoned banners, and the woodland shade,
With leafy flames and dyes autumnal hung,
Makes beautiful the twilight of the year.
For this the fays will dance, for elfin cheer,
Within a dell where some mad girl hath flung
A bracelet that the painted lizards fear—
Red pyres of muffled light! Yet Fancy spurns
The revel, and to eastern hazard turns,
And glaring beacons of the Soldan's shores,
When in a Syrian treasure-house she pours,
From caskets rich and amethystine urns,
Dull fires of dusty jewels that have bound
The brows of naked Ashtaroth around.
Or hushed, at fall of some disastrous night,
When sunset, like a crimson throat to hell,
Is cavernous, she marks the seaward flight

Of homing dragons dark upon the West;
Till, drawn by tales the winds of ocean tell,
And mute amid the splendors of her quest,
To some red city of the Djinns she flees
And, lost in palaces of silence, sees
Within a porphyry crypt the murderous light
Of garnet-crusted lamps whereunder sit
Perturbéd men that tremble at a sound,
And ponder words on ghastly vellum writ,
In vipers' blood, to whispers from the night—
Infernal rubrics, sung to Satan's might,
Or chaunted to the Dragon in his gyre.
But she would blot from memory the sight,
And seeks a stainéd twilight of the South,
Where crafty gnomes with scarlet eyes conspire
To quench Aldebaran's affronting fire,
Low sparkling just beyond their cavern's mouth,
Above a wicked queen's unhallowed tomb.
There lichens brown, incredulous of fame,
Whisper to veinéd flowers her body's shame,
'Mid stillness of all pageantries of bloom.
Within, lurk orbs that graven monsters clasp;
Red-embered rubies smolder in the gloom,
Betrayed by lamps that nurse a sullen flame,
And livid roots writhe in the marble's grasp,
As moaning airs invoke the conquered rust
Of lordly helms made equal in the dust.
Without, where baleful cypresses make rich
The bleeding sun's phantasmagoric gules,
Are fungus-tapers of the twilight witch
(Seen by the bat above unfathomed pools)

And tiger-lilies known to silent ghouls,
Whose king hath digged a somber carcanet
And necklaces with fevered opals set.
But Fancy, well affrighted at his gaze,
Flies to a violet headland of the West,
About whose base the sun-lashed billows blaze,
Ending in precious foam their fatal quest,
As far below the deep-hued ocean molds,
With waters' toil and polished pebbles' fret,
The tiny twilight in the jacinth set,
With wintry orb the moonstone-crystal holds,
Snapt coral twigs and winy agates wet,
Translucencies of jasper, and the folds
Of banded onyx, and vermilion breast
Of cinnabar. Anear on orange sands,
With prows of bronze the sea-stained galleys rest,
And swarthy mariners from alien strands
Stare at the red horizon, for their eyes
Behold a beacon burn on evening skies,
As fed with sanguine oils at touch of night.
Forth from that pharos-flame a radiance flies,
To spill in vinous gleams on ruddy decks;
And overside, when leap the startled waves
And crimson bubbles rise from battle-wrecks,
Unresting hydras wrought of bloody light
Dip to the ocean's phosphorescent caves.

So Fancy's carvel seeks an isle afar,
Led by the Scorpion's rubescent star,
Until in templed zones she smiles to see
Black incense glow, and scarlet-bellied snakes

Sway to the tawny flutes of sorcery.
There priestesses in purple robes hold each
A sultry garnet to the sea-linkt sun,
Or, just before the colored morning shakes
A splendor on the ruby-sanded beach,
Cry unto Betelgeuse a mystic word.
But Fancy, amorous of evening, takes
Her flight to groves whence lustrous rivers run,
Thro' hyacinth, a minster wall to gird,
Where, in the hushed cathedral's jeweled gloom,
Ere Faith return, and azure censers fume,
She kneels, in solemn quietude, to mark
The suppliant day from gorgeous oriels float
And altar-lamps immure the deathless spark;
Till, all her dreams made rich with fervent hues,
She goes to watch, beside a lurid moat,
The kingdoms of the afterglow suffuse
A sentinel mountain stationed toward the night—
Whose broken tombs betray their ghastly trust,
Till bloodshot gems stare up like eyes of lust.
And now she knows, at agate portals bright,
How Circe and her poisons have a home,
Carved in one ruby that a Titan lost,
Where icy philters brim with scarlet foam,
'Mid hiss of oils in burnished caldrons tost,
While thickly from her prey his life-tide drips,
In turbid dyes that tinge her torture-dome;
As craftily she gleans her deadly dews,
With gyving spells not Pluto's queen can use,
Or listens to her victim's moan, and sips
Her darkest wine, and smiles with wicked lips.

Nor comes a god with any power to break
The red alembics whence her gleaming broths
Obscenely fume, as asp or adder froths,
To lethal mists whose writing vapors make
Dim augury, till shapes of men that were
Point, weeping, at tremendous dooms to be,
When pillared pomps and thrones supreme shall stir,
Unstable as the foam-dreams of the sea.

But Fancy still is fugitive, and turns
To caverns where a demon altar burns,
And Satan, yawning on his brazen seat,
Fondles a screaming thing his fiends have flayed,
Ere Lilith come his indolence to greet,
Who leads from hell his whitest queens, arrayed
In chains so heated at their master's fire
That one new-damned had thought their bright attire
Indeed were coral, till the dazzling dance
So terribly that brilliance shall enhance.
But Fancy is unsatisfied, and soon
She seeks the silence of a vaster night,
Where powers of wizardry, with faltering sight
(Whenas the hours creep farthest from the noon)
Seek by the glow-worm's lantern cold and dull
A crimson spider hidden in a skull,
Or search for mottled vines with berries white,
Where waters mutter to the gibbous moon.
There, clothed in cerements of malignant light,
A sick enchantress scans the dark to curse,
Beside a caldron vext with harlot's blood,
The stars of that red Sign which spells her doom.

Then Fancy cleaves the palmy skies adverse
To sunset barriers. By the Ganges' flood
She sees, in her dim temple, Siva loom
And, visioned with the monstrous ruby, glare
On distant twilight where the burning-ghaut
Is lit with glowering pyres that seem the eyes
Of her abhorrent dragon-worms that bear
The pestilence, by Death in darkness wrought.
So Fancy's wings forsake the Asian skies,
And now her heart is curious of halls
In which dead Merlin's prowling ape hath spilt
A vial squat whose scarlet venom crawls
To ciphers bright and terrible, that tell
The sins of demons and the encharneled guilt
That breathes a phantom at whose cry the owl,
Malignly mute above the midnight well,
Is dolorous, and Hecate lifts her cowl
To mutter swift a minatory rune;
And, ere the tomb-thrown echoings have ceased,
The blue-eyed vampire, sated at her feast,
Smiles bloodily against the leprous moon.

But evening now is come, and Fancy folds
Her splendid plumes, nor any longer holds
Adventurous quest o'er stainéd lands and seas—
Fled to a star above the sunset lees,
O'er onyx waters stilled by gorgeous oils
That toward the twilight reach emblazoned coils.
And I, albeit Merlin-sage hath said,
"A vyper lurketh in ye wine-cuppe redde,"

Gaze pensively upon the way she went,
Drink at her font, and smile as one content.

THE ISLANDS OF THE BLEST

In Carmel pines the summer wind
Sings like a distant sea.
O harps of green, your murmurs find
An echoing chord in me!

On Carmel shore the breakers moan
Like pines that breast a gale.
O whence, ye winds and billows, flown
To cry your wordless tale?

Perchance the crimson sunsets drown
In waters whence ye sped;
Perchance the sinking stars go down
To seek the Isles ye fled.

Sometimes from ocean dusks I seem
To glimpse their crystal walls,
Dim jewels of mirage that gleam
In twilight's western halls.

Sometimes I hear below the moon
A music that pursues—
A wraith of melody, that soon
I doubt, and doubting, lose.

Those palmy shores no prow may find,
But once it seemed to me
A ghost of fragrance roamed the wind.
Yet was not of the sea.

What tho' my tale the seaman scorns?
The Chart of Dreams, unrolled,
Attests their haven's jasper bourns,
Their reefs of sunken gold.

I do not know what lonely strands
Await the wingéd star;
I only know their evening sands
Seem wonderful and far.

THE LOVER WAITS

This her home! And oh, my homeless heart!
Mine eyes fill, for I know that yonder light
Assures her loveliness to other eyes. . . .
The stars go down. I hear the whimpering owl,
And little winds go past me in the dark,
Softly, afraid to wake the drowsing oaks
That guard her home with rough but faithful breasts.
Ah me! that mine were sleeping at their roots—
Too still to fear, as now, her smallest scorn.
The dews descend. The breath of flowers that die
Ascends. They mingle in the tender night
To some faint, holy symbol of her soul. . . .
The rose must pass, the starlight of the dew. . . .
There's little comfort in the stars to-night,
Tho' Venus o'er the mountain, glows like fire
Split from the censer of the Pleiades. . . .
I think this waiting will wear out my heart;
But ever 't was, that he who loves must wait—
'T is part of all Love's hunger, nor would I
Forego one gleam of his irradiant wings:
His pains are sweeter than another's joy. . . .
The stars to-night seem curious, and peer
Beyond the unstirring leaves, as tho' to say:
"Lover, alas! we've seen all this before,
And know the silence that must end it all."
But they—the night of God shall still them each
Who give me now their pity or their scorn,
And deem that loves is naught because it dies.

Little they know the wings that wait its Dream!
I'd sift the constellations for her brow,
To leave her crowned forever. Foolish lights,
I tell you that her eyes are Love's despair,
And all her beauty pain for very gods,
So fair is she! But she will not come forth
And let my heart forget that you exist
Or land or sea—only that Eden's mine,
And she and I alone. . . . Now I'll dream
That some great rose has died, and that its soul
Goes by me on the night—goes by to God,
Who has all beauty in His gift, and gave
More to my Sweet than to the flowers she loves!
'T is true she thinks me mad, nor yet believes
What chains mine eyes have fashioned for my heart,
Deeming that it should fathom first her own
And find what's there: I scorn so cautious love!
Better delusion than a heart that plots,
And chaffers first with Love to find the cost:
I'll fence with Death, but Love shall have me blind.
Yet 't is as well that woman's breast should house
The inherited Misgiving. Still for her
Love is too oft a sexton at the last. . . .
Thank God there is no moon to make me ghosts
Among the blossoms of the orchard-trees!
For I've my dead—few, but a sleepless lot.
'T is only woman living makes one wait
And question all one's stars. Ye trees, there's that
Your roots cannot detain. A truce to this!
Shall night enmingle with my very blood—
And such a night? But listen, O ye trees!

Are those her footfalls, or my leaping heart?

TO EDGAR ALLAN POE

Time, who but jests with sword and sovereignty,
   Confirming these as phantoms in his gloom
   Or bubbles that his arid hours consume,
Shall mold an undeparting light of thee—
A star whereby futurity shall see
   How Song's eventual majesties illume,
   Beyond Augustan pomp or battle-doom,
Her annals of abiding heraldry.

Time, tho' his mordant ages gnaw the crag,
   Shall blot no hue from thy seraphic wings
     Nor vex thy crown and choral glories won,
Albeit the solvents of Oblivion drag
   To dust the sundered sepulchers of kings,
     In desolations splendid with the sun.

IN EXTREMIS

Till dawn the Winds' insuperable throng
    Passed over like archangels in their might,
    With roar of chariots from their stormy height,
And broken thunder of mysterious song—
By mariner or sentry heard along
    The star-usurping battlements of night—
    And wafture of immeasurable flight,
And high-blown trumpets muntinous and strong.

Till Louder on the dreadful dark I heard
    The shrieking of the tempest-tortured tree,
      And deeper on immensity the call
    And tumult of the empire-forging sea;
But near the eternal Peace I lay, nor stirred,
    Knowing the happy dead hear not at all.

ROMANCE

Thou passest, and we know thee not, Romance!
  Thy gaze is backward, and thy heart is fed
  With murmurs and with music of the dead.
Alas, our battle! for the rays that glance
On thy dethroning sword and haughty lance
  Are of forgotten suns and stars long fled;
  Thou weavest phantom roses for thy head,
And ghostly queens in thy dominion dance.

Would we might follow thy returning wings,
  And in thy farthest haven beach our prow—
    Thy dragons conquered and thine oceans
        crossed—
And find thee standing on the dust of kings,
  A lion at thy side, and on thy brow
  The light of sunsets wonderful and lost!

THE FOREST MOTHER

Athlon the king bade silence to his harps,
Which murmured for a little, and were mute.
Then, gazing shrewdly on his men-of-war,
Whose armor, scattered in the banquet-hall,
Cast back the lurching torch-light, hoarsely spake:
"Methinks where War drew bronze athwart your
        cheeks
Love hath sown lilies, and your sinews shrink,
Lax with the feast. And not with lutes and wine
Won ye my strongholds and the guarded hills.
Your horses please you not, but daintier steeds,
And strife of happy loins. So grow ye soft.
Wherefore, this month, when dawn beholds the moon
A ghost, I call your swords to cleaner war,
To peril, and high battle with its toils.
But lest ye think I chide unwitting, list!
I tell a happening of younger years.
"I, Athlon, as ye know, be mountain-born,
And suckled at the torrent. Of our blood
Was never sage nor priest. Not seaward roamed
A stormier breed. Nor is it strange we wrought
Ever to-north dominion, and with steel,
And herald arrow whispering our law,
Pushed out our straining borders, till at last
Corvannon fell, and all our foeman's line.
Thereafter, my red father at that sack
Being fallen, I was king, and held my state
In Gurth his treasure-city. Such the fear
Our lances bred, that for a prudent space

The land had quiet, while with crafts and lore
I labored, and was Beauty's servitor
In pleasant places, being likewise chief
Of wary councils, and with cunning pact,
Statecraft, and grey disposal of mine arts
Wrought kingship. As the elder of you learnt,
I made carousal nightly, and was long
At banqueting, and amorous, for these
Were joys witholden from my youth. Wherefore
The days ran merrily. At times, forsooth,
My captains craved incitements of old war,
But I constrained their furies. Then they held
Hot tournament, and vigors of the chase;
Yet would I none of these, but month by month,
Sat slothful, wasting me my needful nights
With wine and transient loves. I grew o'erfond
Of luscious viands, and did hold my fool
Above mine armorer. For silken robes
I bargained often with sea-faring men,
And drowsed o'er written tales. So flew my years.

"One summer, when a people had been bold,
My border guards made foray. Of their spoil
Was little precious save a splendid girl,
Held to my pleasure. Wherefore, late one eve,
I sought her vigiled chamber. At my touch,
His yellow-haired barbarian of the hills,
Upstarting, flung me from her scornful breast.
Young-bosomed, virginal, she stood and laughed,
(A mountain-eagle glorious in her strength),
Held my desire at arm's-length, and made mock

At me, so fain to close with her. Behold!
She stood the stronger! Sneering then, she cried:
'Thine eyes are sick! Thy breath is foul with wine!
Go nest thee with thy harlots! Soft thy limbs—
Kiss softer, an thou find'st them! Northern mail
Would flay thy skin, and outland winds thy cheek!
Get hither!' I, remembering past might—
How once I could have held her helpless—raged,
Yet in the end departed, vainly wroth.

"Then thought I of my mother of the hills,
Of that calm strength wherefrom mine own had birth,
Her hands so blest with healing, and her lips
Silent with wisdom. Yea! I would go forth,
Regain that younger home, abide in peace,
And haunt the quietude of ancient woods,
Then seek my city even as once I came,
The war-horse mad beneath me, in my grasp
The shearing axe, and on my head the helm,
Red-gleaming like Arcturus ere he mount
The midnight, when the rain has washed the dark.

"So sought I then my mother's dwelling. She,
Whom other sons had sorrowed, gazed awhile,
And smiling sadly at the lines that Love
And Care had graven, told me all her mind,
Speaking me plain, who was no king to her,
But greedy Athlon, pertest of her brood.

"Thereafter I was guardian and serf
Of that grey house; did hew and draw, did face

Those vaster hills, and swam their coldest streams.
I harried fierce their wild and furry kind,
And sought me mountain sunsets, and the dawn,
Seen beyond eastern snows. My counsellors
Were learnéd trees, wise-whispering. I grew
As rough as they, as kindly. Their domain
Was fair with holy twilights and the hush
Of night long-lingering. About their feet
The brook remembered legends of their youth,
And younger dawnings. Fitfully they mourned,
Responsive, as the unreturning wind
Cried from their mighty heart-strings, and the dusk
Found kindred voices. Well my mother knew
The hurts of men, what balms had gentlest touch
And wrought the cleanlier. She, faithful, loved
The man within that form which cities shape,
And knew his follies. When I fain had kissed
Her serving-maids, she laughed aloud and said:
'Haste hillward, son, and hug the willing bear!'
And when my hands would steal her cellared wine,
(The blood of niggard slopes), she said: 'Drink first
Our upland lake, fed sweet from distant snows.
That gone, thou shalt have darker vintage.' I,
So counselled, stood a-grin like any oaf.

"Thus with her pure medicaments she wrought;
Then, when the pulse had slacked and sinews drawn,
And saner blood wrought morning on my face,
She said: 'Go hence, my boy, for noble cares
Await thee, and the duties of the crown.
Yet stay not always in thy courts, but come

Often, and seek the music of my home,
Its dews and shadows, fragrances and calm,
Its moonlight, and the stars that watch thy sleep.'
So came I to my halls, and her that dwelt
Therein, well-guarded by my sentinels."

Thus spake the king, and signalled to his harps;
But swiftly on the silence that was come,
"Didst master her?" cried one among his lords.
To whom the king, rem'niscent in his beard:
"In twenty years she gat me nine great sons,
Greedy for battle." Then, with mournful voice,
"Our other nine were daughters," quoth the king.

A VIOLET

Thee, of her frail and tender brood
    Frailest and tenderest,
Earth holds (prophetic motherhood!)
    The closest to her breast.

THE WILD IRIS

Afar the silent clouds go by,
And snows of cloud and stain of sky
Within my lowly bosom lie.

The heedless sky unchanging stands;
The clouds drift on to distant lands;
Man comes and takes me in his hands.

We pass. The lonely heavens abide.
From gulfs unknown that mock his pride
He turns to see me at his side.

What stirs him so he can not say:
I stand along his troubled way
No less a mystery than they.

Kin to the mortal flower that grows
To fade, he droops at last; he goes
To deeper peace than Nature knows.

'T is meet I share his rest, for he,
Alone of living things that be
Of earth, has given love to me.

TO AN ELDER POET

Now stir the blossoms in the grass;
　　But oh! the fadeless flowers you bring
　　Are children of a wilder Spring,
And pass not tho' the seasons pass.

Their breath along the Singing-Way
　　　Is more of rapture than of rest;
　　　The undeparting blooms attest
What rains and winds of yesterday!

THE HOMING OF THE DRAKE

DRAKE'S BAY, SEPTEMBER 29, 1579.

Was it the night that foiled his daring eyes,
Or passed he in the blindness of the fog
To-south, nor dreamt what keep of empire stood
So near his grasp? I can but deem it strange
That God withheld from England in that hour
The incomparable haven, that His veils
Were somehow on the insatiate sight of Drake,
So that the land is not to-day her dow'r —
She, fostered since by all His winds and tides!
For then, as now, the Port lay vast with peace,
The hills were wardens of the far-sought gold,
And streams were glad in valleys unprofaned,
Rich as that France she harried. Had he seen,
In time his tale had set her out-post here,
Guard of the coast forever. But his eyes
Were holden, and our waters checked him not—
For leagues beyond the grey and desolate Gate
Stained from swart rivers! Saw he not the clue? —
Nay, blind to empire sundered from his sight,
He passed, the intrepid, and the Golden Hind,
A waif in hostile deserts of the deep,
Fled homeward, to such issues as are told,
When but a glance, or quickening of the sense,
Had shattered thrones, and rent the bourns of rule,
And broken crownéd fames, and swerved the course
Of all the tides of conquest round the world.

The Fates have mighty darkness at their seats,

Nor use revealing stars. Wherefore to us
Time's sea is strange, nor learn we to what Law
Our needle veers, nor witness, for the Dark,
What Shapes inscrutable stand at the helm,
Nor whence (amazed) the ordaining winds that urge
Our keels to harbors other than we dream.

THE CLOUD

Said the cloud, "I am weary of flight
    And the wind's imperious reign:
I will foil forever his might;
    I will rest from striving and pain;
I will pass to the peace of night."

And she sank in rain to the mead;
    But her tears were life to the lands,
And she came as a voice to the seed,
    And she came with weal in her hands
To the fainting flower's need.

In the secret caverns of earth,
    In the groping veins of the soil,
She fashioned the dust of dearth,
    In faith and vision of toil,
To the harvest of Autumn's mirth.

Her strength was holden and tried,
    Her heart to service was true,
Till the roots of the grass were guide
To the day's remembered blue,
Where the winds of Spring were wide.

And she spread her wings to the sun,
    And she rose again on the air,
Till her wings with the light were one
    In a sunset strange and fair,
Where the winds forever run.

THREE SONNETS ON OBLIVION

Dedicated to Mr. Raphael Weill

I - OBLIVION

Her eyes have seen the monoliths of kings
    Upcast like foam of the effacing tide;
    She hath beheld the desert stars deride
The monuments of Power's imaginings —
About their base the wind Assyrian flings
    The dust that throned the satrap in his pride;
    Cambyses and the Memphian pomps abide
As in the flame the moth's presumptuous wings.

There gleams no glory that her hand shall spare,
    Nor any sun whose rays shall cross her night,
        Whose realm enfolds man's empire and its end.
No armor of renown her sword shall dare,
    No council of the gods withstand her might:
        Stricken at last Time's lonely Titans bend.

THREE SONNETS ON OBLIVION

II - THE DUST DETHRONED

Sargon is dust, Semiramis a clod!
   In crypts profaned the moon at midnight peers;
   The owl upon the Sphinx hoots in her ears,
And scant and sear the desert grasses nod
Where once the armies of Assyria trod,
   With younger sunlight splendid on the spears;
   The lichens cling the closer with the years,
And seal the eyelids of the weary god.

Where high the tombs of royal Egypt heave,
   The vulture shadows with arrested wings
   The indecipherable boasts of kings,
     As Arab children hear their mother's cry
And leave in mockery their toy — they leave
   The skull of Pharaoh staring at the sky.

THREE SONNETS ON OBLIVION

III - THE NIGHT OF GODS

Their mouths have drunken the eternal wine —
   The draught that Baal in oblivion sips.
   Unseen about their courts the adder slips,
Unheard the sucklings of the leopard whine;
The toad has found a resting-place divine
   And bloats in stupor between Amnion's lips.
   O Carthage and the unreturning ships,
The fallen pinnacle, the shifting Sign!

Lo! when I hear from voiceless court and fane
   Time's adoration of Eternity —
      The cry of kingdoms past and gods undone—
I stand as one whose feet at noontide gain
   A lonely shore; who feels his soul set free,
      And hears the blind sea chanting to the sun.

HELEN PETERSON

DIED AGED SEVEN

We question not what Faith beholds,
　　Nor mix farewell with prayer,
As now Eternity enfolds
　　What Time beheld so fair:
Sinless as any flower we bring
　　Art thou whom Heaven gave;
Death never touched a gentler thing
　　Than thou whose peace we crave.

Here half-consoled we kiss thy brow
　　(We cannot speak our tears)
In gratitude at least that thou
　　Hast foiled the sadder years,
Hast fled the years when care and pain
　　Would greet thine elder breath,
To sleep forever without stain,
　　How innocent in death!

Beyond our clasp thy soul must wait,
　　Wiser than we at last,
Till each attain, in peace as great,
　　The silence that thou hast;
Be then it given each to be
　　What now in truth thou art —
Pure love renewed by memory
　　In twilights of the heart.

TASSO TO LEONORA

FOREWORD

For his declaration of love to Leonora d'Este (sister of his patron, Alfonso II, Duke of Ferrara), Torquato Tasso, one of the four great poets of Italy, was confined for seven years as a madman in the hospital of St Anne, by order of the duke. Leonora died on February the tenth, 1581, five years before his release.

Because he wanders lonely, without hope,
Because supreme despair hath slain his dream,
Love, for his very hopelessness, makes cry,
Living to thee a little as a voice.

I know not if thy heart can ever turn
To one unworthy. Thy disdain, perchance,
May come, and with unfaltering touch reveal
The might of chords that in the spirit thrill
To pain. And yet I cannot guard my lips
Forever. Comes this hush about the soul
But for love's whisper: listen ere it pass.

Thou seemest farther from me than a star,
The morning star, that hovers like a flame
Above the great dawn-altar. So for this,
Thy terrible remoteness, must I speak.
And purer thou and sweeter than a wind
Whose wings, caught in an Eden of the rose,
Win through its maze aweary. So for this,
Thy purity and sweetness, must I speak.
Because of all the wonder that thou art
I cry my love, lest suddenly great Death
Go mad for thee, and kiss thy lips too soon.

And for the very frailty of this life
I cry my love. For as the abiding sea
Transpires a tiny firmament of foam
That, quivering, mirrors for a space the abyss
Which was its font, and that which takes its soul,
So gleams mortality, a trembling film
Between the deep within and deep without.

I, fearful lest thou take the eternal ways
And know not I remain a lonely fire
Within the night thou leavest, call to thee.

Never had lover's dusk such moon as thou!
Never had moon adoring such as mine!
For at thy spirit in her majesty
Mine own is greatly humbled, and forgets
Its haughtiness, forsaking at thy feet
Song's archangelic panoply of light,
And sits a child before thee, and is glad.
Yea, though I deem the silences of love
More beautiful than music, or the hush
Of ocean twilights, yet my soul to thine
Swoons deaf and blind, with living lips that ache
And cry to thee its joy and wonderment.
I would that I were morning to thine eyes!
I would that I were honey in thy mouth!
I would I might thrill through thee as delight,
And might in fragrance of immortal flow'rs
Besiege thee, and might take all cadences
Of riven waters and of crying chords,
The voice of bird and wind and threnody,

The deep's slow thunder, and the murmurings
Of fire, and might enthrall and mingle these,
And live to thee in music! Even thus
I, Tasso, calling from my throne of pain,
Would fathom thee, who art unfathomable,
And as a sky my love would compass thee,
Who art illimitable. Ah, low voice,
Heard above all the voices of the day!
Ah, face imperative as sleep, that night
Orbs to a star, and mingles with my dreams!
Ah, high despair, and hope of him whose hope
Is but to clasp thy spirit after death!
Though death draw down this body, still my soul—
A song between its dawn and eve of time —
Shall turn to thee for memory, and lose,
Unwept, all meed of evanescent joy,
With thee its heritage. And though thy world,
A-storm in all its citadels and courts,
Bear thee beyond me, yet its darkened might
Gives but new might to yearning. Yea, though hell
Arch over me its hurricanes of fire,
Still shall I love, nor falter, standing true
To that pure light whereof thou abidest shrine,
For which all else is dark, mine eyes being fixed
Alway thereon. Yet not as they that find
Love tenderness, and sweet with pitying lips,
Find I his glories, but a thing of flame,
And with fierce mien forbidding, and with eyes
Inexorable, calm with all disdain,
And with ungracious hands, and threatening wings,
Sad for their cruel splendor. Yet his voice

Calls but thy name unceasingly — thy name,
An echo in the abysses of the heart,
That rests a time, now having found its realm
All deeps and exaltations of unrest. . . .

Ah, peace for but a little! I awake,
And now again my heart is made a world
Wherein the Titans, Rapture and Despair,
Do battle each with each. Thou swayest them,
Who art the swift fulfilment of all dreams
Of love in loneliness — ideals mute
The mind uplifts for worshiping. Thy face
Restores lost visions of Hellenic nights
And all their moons that perished. Nymph and
          queen
Live in thee: thou art that Persephone —
Torn from the clasping day — whose maiden eyes,
'Mid one deep murmur of Plutonian harps,
Greatened in retrospection. Daphne thou;
Psyche that waits her lover in the night;
Calypso and the luring of her lyres.

Nay! Thou art more than these, howbeit their souls
Stir in thee. In humility I come,
I call, I pray, O whiter than the snows
Of orient and cloudland cold with dawn!
Thy light is from afar, and thine the heights
The stainless know. Ah I fallen from its skies,
My darker soul calls from its distances
And shadows unendurable. Judge thou
Its worship, and the hunger thou hast made,

That I, from darkness and my little worth,
Dare tell thee my adoring. But I wait,
And dawn comes drifting on its golden tides,
Or dawn comes later from reluctant mist,
Yet thou a stranger still to me, and night
Comes, though it brings not slumber, yet no voice
In me a desert. And the barren years
Darken beyond us, and the silence grows
Unto a mystery foreshadowing
The sorrows of the world. Eternity
Draws nearer with its answers, and I seem
A wandering echo in the night of Change,
The ghost of something futile and forgot,
A star lost from the sister lights. Unrest
Gives me thy face for slumber, and the day
Thy destinies as dream. And memory
Strives backward for thee to the dark of birth,
And seeks the light of antenatal life —
Finding thee almost, for thy haunting face
Thrills with the rose of unremembered dawns,
Thine eyes hold azure of a younger sea,
The depths of thine incomparable hair
Twilights in which we parted, and thy voice
The grief and music of forgotten lives.

It may be that my lips shall never touch
The cup of love brimmed with its quivering wine;
Yet sit I crowned, splendor invisible
Upon me, happy that I turn from Time
Holding one dream found perfect. It may be,
As now, that until death my yearning arms

Shall seek thee only in dream-paradise,
O pearl of oceans infinite! that Love
Sit alway in unchanging solitude,
And call unheard; that nightward thou wilt turn,
Nor wilt remember, save for pitying,
My world left mist and ashes. Still my soul
Hath known thee, and may summon: Memory,
Life's shadow, holds forever at her heart
The beautiful that passeth. I am glad,
And, homeless for Eternity, have rest
In thee for Time. Had I thy very scorn,
Yet were I richer, and might smile in tears,
Clasping the pain immortal things must know.
Think not my lips would harm thee: all my heart
Trembles to thine, and, rather far than Love
Found sorrow or nepenthe, at thy feet
Would lie as dust that gathered to a rose,
And died in silence, and was dust again.

OF AMERICA

JANUARY 1ST, 1908

Cry some, in seeming wisdom of the hour:
"Not Babylon, nor Karnak in her pomp,
Knew fairer paths to doom than thou. Thy skies
Are gentleness. Incessantly the Fates
Hold thee in kindest scrutiny. Thy feet
Tread sunward, God being wroth with thee at last,
Alloting thee no more His sterner ways
And cleanly times of war. For now He grants
The recompense of battle — pleasant years,
And such reward as age discerns. Grown soft,
Thy hands reach out for mercenary joys;
Thy heart desires dishonorable loves
And baser dreams. Yearly the golden chain
Is weightier at thy wrists, and fostered Pow'rs
Plan in their dusk of tyranny thy tomb;
And in that shadow Mammon's eyes grow fierce,
And half thy sons adore him. Now the land
Grows vile, and all thy statehood is a mart. . . .
So passed the elder empires. So thy might—
thou too bléssed in immediate wealth! —
Ebbs with the day, till night behold thy doom,
Nor feels the menace of that lethal time
When sinks the day-star of senescent realms,
Slow-westering in splendors of decay."

Let men arraign thy worth; yet Man has found
Till now no ampler heavens than thine, nor years

Made safe for purer purpose to the race.
Our fathers builded well, and tho' our walls,
To children of the fairer days to come,
Be seen the least foundation of the plinth
Wherefrom, assoiled, our sons to be shall rear
That final Temple to confront the skies,
Nathless, to each his own, to every age
Its war: their dust is equal at the last!
And thou, thou hast the daylight still in dow'r;
The dews are young upon thy leafy crown;
We love thee for thy youth, believing still
That nobler mornings wait thy sovereign eyes;
That Time, in expiation, yet shall crown
The sordid years with Brotherhood, and we
Walk sane at last, nor strive as wolves or swine
Each for his glut, and heedless each of all.
We trust thy Fates, nor dread the hidden years,
Beholding radiance about thy brow —
Beautiful light, whose rays reveal thy strength,
And yet shall consecrate that strength to Man.

Thus hope we, though the vatic past appal,
And Wisdom whisper but dismay; so trust,
Being as voyagers whose mist-held eyne
See not the Star, yet know the Star abides.

BEAUTY

The fairest things seem ever loneliest:
    The whitest lily ever blooms alone,
    And purest winds from widest seas are flown.
High on her utmost tower of the West
Sits Beauty, baffling an eternal quest;
    From out her gates and oriels unknown
    The murmurs of her citadels are blown
To blue horizons of the world's unrest.

We know that we shall seek her till we die,
    And find her not at all, the fair and far:
Her pure domain is wider than the sky,
    And never night revealed her whitest star;
        Beyond the sea and sun her feet have trod;
        Her vision is our memory of God.

THE SOUL PRISMATIC

Forlorn, as twilight saddens now the hills,
    I gaze across the dim and lonely plain
    And muse, till musing is at last a pain,
On all the voices of the countless rills,
On all the loveliness unseen that fills
    The mountains — hidden beauty lost like rain
    On wastes of the unalterable main;
Lost, as a music that the midnight stills.

God I for a heart to make it so mine own
    That I would be as crystals that accept
    Most marvelously the concealing ray;
Till on my page in splendor should be thrown
    Such revelation as of hues that slept,
    Unheeded, in the clarity of day!

PRIDE AND CONSCIENCE

Considering the mystery of pain,
   I walked one day, when lo! in rags awry,
   Awrench and gnarled, a hunchback shambled by;
Whereat, "In what far certitude of gain
Dost Thou debase Thine image, and disdain
   Our hearts that love the beautiful?" asked I.
   "Wilt Thou in Thy derision, O Most High!
Like kings of old keep monsters in Thy train?"

Also I said, "The shadows of Thy whole
   And dreadful plan are witness of the light,
     And strict concern of relativity."
   So came, unerring as the sunbeam's flight,
The indignant challenge of mine undersoul:
     "Nay! who is straight in God's sight — thou
        or he?"

AN APRIL MORNING

Slow to the wanton sun's desire
   The vestal-bosomed buds unfold,
Till poppies flaunt a silken fire,
   And buttercups a glassy gold.

How gently fare the cloudy flocks
   To pastures girdled by the seal
The lizards twitch along the rocks,
   And subtle odors lure the bee.

There broods a peace upon the hills,
   Too vast for morning winds to break,
Tho' murmurs throng the broken rills,
   And voices of the woodland wake,

Till half I turn to hear again
   The flutes of Arcady at dawn,
And rout of hurrying nymphs that feign
   To dread the kisses of the faun.

THE SIREN'S SONG

FROM "DUANDON"

Far down, where virgin silence reigns,
    In jasper evenings of the sea,
    I toss my pearls, I wait for thee.
The sea hath lent me all its stains:
    It is but treasure-house of me.

The corals of the sea have caught
    A Titan shell whose fragile dome
    Is crimson o'er mine ocean home,
Mine opal chambers subtly wrought
    In semblance of the shaken foam.

Oh! come! and thou shalt dream with me
    By violet foam at twilight tost
    On strands of ocean islets lost
To prows that seek them wearily,
    O'er seas by questing sunsets crost.

All dreams that Hope hath promised Love,
    All beauty thou hast sought in vain,
    All joy held once and lost again,
These, and the mystery thereof,
    I guard beneath the sundering main.

MADRIGAL

Maiden, doff thy dream, and rise!
Morning's rose is in the skies;
In the meadow I can hear
Birds in chorus crystal-clear.

Maiden, rise, and fare with me
Where expectant flowers be —
Blossoms holding thee in hope:
When thou comest, they will ope.

What to me is any bird,
If it sing by thee unheard?
What is any lovely spot,
If its blossoms know thee not?

TO INA COOLBRITH

With wilder sighing in the pine
   The wind went by, and so I dreamed;
   And in that dusk of sleep it seemed
A city by the sea was mine.

No statelier sprang the walls of Tyre
   From seaward cliff or palaced hill;
   And light and music met to fill
The splendid courts of her desire —

(Extolling chords that cried her praise,
   And golden reeds whose mellow moan
   Was like an ocean's undertone
Dying and lost on forest ways.)

But sweeter far than any sound
   That rang or rippled in her halls,
   Was one beyond her eastern walls,
By summer gardens girdled round.

'Twas from a nightingale, and oh!
   The song it sang hath never word!
   Sweeter it seemed than Love's, first-heard,
Or lutes in Aidenn murmuring low.

Faint, as when drowsy winds awake
   A sisterhood of faery bells,
   It won reply from hidden dells,

Loyal to Echo for its sake. . . .

I dreamt I slept, but cannot say
　　How many dreamland seasons fled,
　　Nor what horizon of the dead
Gave back my dream's uncertain day.

But still beside the toiling sea
　　I lay, and saw — for walls o'ergrown—
　　The city that was mine had known
Time's sure and ancient treachery.

Above her ramparts, broad as Tyre's,
　　The grasses' mounting army broke;
　　The shadows of the sprawling oak
Usurpt the splendor of her fires.

But o'er the fallen marbles pale
　　I heard, like elfin melodies
　　Blown over from enchanted seas,
The music of the nightingale.

A MOOD

I am grown weary of permitted things
    And weary of the care-emburdened age —
    Of any dusty lore of priest and sage
To which no memory of Arcadia clings;
For subtly in my blood at evening sings
    A madness of the faun — a choric rage
    That makes all earth and sky seem but a cage
In which the spirit pines with cheated wings.

Rather by dusk for Lilith would I wait
    And for a moment's rapture welcome death,
Knowing that I had baffled Time and Fate,
      And feeling on my lips, that died with day
    As sense and soul were gathered to a breath,
      The immortal, deadly lips that kissing slay.

A VISITOR

The winter twilight and the mournful rain
Were one, and on the pavements of the town
The lights fell wet. Betimes the darkness came,
And came a headlong wind from out the South,
That plucked upon the dripping wires, and fled,
Affrighted at its harping. Night and storm
Made drearier the solitary streets,
And whining cars cast clamors on the dark.

But warm within their home Elaine and John
Sat by their fire, that round the pleasant room
Threw wincing shadows, or with restless gleams
Lit up a vase or book or patient clock,
Those placid friends we gather with the years,
Nor which outgrow us. Stern without, the wind
Spoke in some tree, but they spoke not at all,
Because between their hearts was made that rift
Which, opening at times to most who love,
Ere long is closed, yet which perchance may gape,
And widen with the days, and deepen down,
Till some two gaze across a bridgeless gulf
At eyes grown strangers. So the unwearied wind
Moaned, and the rain was harsh upon the roof,
And John reread the news, till mute Elaine,
Her eyes grown tired with gazing at the fire,
Saw half its glowing temples fall to ash.

Then, on that bitter silence of their pride,

There came a knock, not timid. John arose
And lit their little hall, and turned the knob:
A man stood tall without, with haughty face,
And costly garments proof against the rain.
Then John: "Come in." At which the stranger shook
From all his height the silver of the storm,
And bared his head, and entered. Then, with mind
Grown curious, said John: "What can I do?"
"I only ask," their guest replied, "to walk
About your home." Thereat some parleying
Ensued, for tho' 'twas old — a rented roof,
A cottage mossed by many winters gone —
They cherished it, not wished remove therefrom.
But soon relenting, John arose, and lit
Their six small rooms, and at the stranger's side
Was usher, telling, needlessly perhaps,
The use of each. In one the light was low,
And gentlest breathing told of childhood's sleep—
Their guest paused longest there. But in each room
He paused, and said no word, while loud without
Echoed the storm, as hurrying from the South
The rain's grey army passed. Then hastily
He said: "I thank you," turned, a moment stood,
And went out silent to the cloven night.
But they two ran, re-opening the door
(Wistful to call him back), and saw his form
Descend the steps, and heard a grievous cry
From out the dark: "Here I was happy once!"
And they two turned, and kissed in sudden tears.

A DREAM OF FEAR

Unseen the ghostly hand that led,
   I walked where all was darkness, save
   What light the moon, half-wasted, gave
Above a city of the dead.

So lone it was, so grey, I deemed
   That death itself was scarce so old;
   The moonlight fell forlorn and cold
On tombs where Time lay dead, it seemed.

Within its gates I heard the sound
   Of winds in cypress-caverns caught
   Of huddling trees that moaned, and sought
To whisper what their roots had found.

Within its gates my soul was led,
   Down nettle-choked and haunted way—
   An atom of the Dark's dismay,
In deaf immensities of dread.

In broken crypts where ghouls had slept
   I saw how muttering devils sate
   (Knowing the final grasp of Fate)
And told grim auguries, and wept.

The night was mad with nameless fear.
   The Powers of Darkness feared the gloom.
   From sentried sky to anxious tomb

Ran messages I bent to hear.

Mine ears were sealed, nor heard I save
   The secret known to Endor's witch —
   Whispered to lemur and to lich
From lips made wiser by the grave.

O'er tarns where spectral vapors flowed
   Antares shook with bloody light,
   And guarded on its haughty flight
The offended fire of Alphard glowed.

The menace of infinity
   Constrained the cavern of the skies.
   I felt the gaze of solemn eyes
In hostile gulfs intent to see;

Gage of whose imminent designs,
   Satanic Armageddon broke,
   Where monstrous vans in blackness spoke
The flight of Evil on the Signs —

Abysmal occultation cast
   By kingdoms of the sunken noon,
   And shadow-shafts that smote the moon
At altars of the cloven Vast!

To worlds that faltered on their way
   Python's intolerable hiss
   Told from the jaws of his abyss
Malign amazement and dismay.

By god or demon undestroyed,
   In malediction sate the stars,
   Concentered from Titanic wars
To cry the judgments of the Void.

Assigned, implacable, supreme,
   The heralds of the Curse came down:
   I felt the eternal bastions' frown;
I saw colossal cerements gleam.

Convoking trumpets shook the gloom.
   Their incommunicable word
   Announced o'er Time's foundations, stirred.
All vasts and covenants of doom.

I saw the light of dreadful fanes,
   I heard enormous valves resound,
   For aeons sealed in crypts profound,
And clangor of ascending chains.

NIGHT IN HEAVEN

All the harps of Heaven sang in the timeless noon-
       tide,
Sang in the day that God had made eternity;
And memory was fled at the drying of the tears,
    Tears that won the Happiness.

Many in their bliss were the souls that had for-
       gotten —
Souls lost in light that hid them each from each;
And their harping as a sea beat on the Throne
      unceasingly,
    Joyous and terrible.
And vaster from their chords surged the music made
      marvelous,
Till they sang not as men whom He saved for their
      lowliness;
Till their quiring was as that of the angels who
      sinned not,
Familiar of His glory.

And the Lord thought, "Behold I they are yet as
      wayward children,
Forgetful with joy, and haughty in their music!
Now shall I cause that their hearts renew their need
      of Me,
    And one of another."

All the harps of Heaven sang in a sudden twilight,

And the souls gazed each on each in the ebbing of
          His radiance;
Low throbbed the chords till their music was of
          memory
     And the homes of theirs sorrow-time.
They sang of toil that ceased, and of kine that left
          the hillside,
Of dumb things that fed, and of children tired
          and dusty,
Of the moon great and low, and the warmth of lowly
          hearths —
     These, and their comforting.

All the harps of Heaven sang in a holy darkness,
And like the stars in dew shone the tears of men
          remembering,
Weary men and humble, that had the night for
          slumber —
     Night and its tenderness.

Now if they forget, and the human in their harping
Cease like a flower from the face of things eternal,
Comes again the evening, the shadow of His glory.
     So the souls remember.

PERSONAL SONNETS

Goddess of hearts by beauty's right divine,
   If yet in any isle of ancient seas
   Or garden of the lost Hesperides
An altar to the Cytherean shine,
Go thou not thither, tho' the gods repine;
   But grant us, we that love thy dear decrees,
   To know thy sway — solicitous to please
With coronals and sacrificial wine.

Permit us that the dove-voiced flutes extol
   Thy grace, and ours be garlands that enthrall
   Of sacred myrtle to thy service grown.
Beauty hath many pathways to the soul,
   And thou, O gentle queen, hast found them all,
   Making each heart thou enterest thy throne.

PERSONAL SONNETS

Master, when worms have had their will of thee,
   And thou art but a voice along the years —
   A star in the companionship of spheres
That are Fame's firmament — may God decree
That song and song's hostilities shall be
   A sword within my hands, a flame that sears
   The liar's mouth that slanders thee, nor fears
The vengeances of Truth's supremacy!

O Fates that on the tomb of greatness dead
   Permit the viper and the toad to bask,
     Lend me your youngest lightnings, and impel
   My spirit as a whirlwind to the task
To char the liar's tongue within his head —
     Like ashes on the adamant of Hell!

PERSONAL SONNETS

III- NORA MAY FRENCH

I saw the shaken stars of midnight stir,
  And winds that sought the morning bore to me
  The thunder where the legions of the sea
Are shattered on her stormy sepulcher,
And pondering on bitter things that were,
  On cruelties the mindless Fates decree,
  I felt some shadow of her mystery —
The loneliness and mystery of her.

The waves that break on undiscovered strands,
  The winds that die on seas that bear no sail,
  Stars that the deaf, eternal skies annul,
Were not so lonely as was she. Our hands
  We reach tathee from Time — without avail,
  O spirit mighty and inscrutable!

PERSONAL SONNETS

SCULPTOR

The abiding marble shadows forth thy dream;
    But in what quarries of infinity
    Must spirit strive with formlessness to free
The vision? Lo! upon the mind's extreme
It bursts from darkness like a dawn supreme —
    The rainbow of an undiscovered sea,
    A blossom of that vine of mystery
Whose roots touch night, whose flowers in morning
        gleam.

We are but thoughts. With music or the pen
    We tell what silences about us brood,
        And limn with masteries of hue or stone,
Set for a little in the sight of men,
    The visions of that mighty solitude
        From which we come, to which we pass, *alone!*

PERSONAL SONNETS

V - TO CHARLES ROLLO PETERS

MASTER-PAINTER OF NOCTURNES

The padres have departed from our lands,
   And gone with them is all their gentler lore;
   The mission bells waft yet, beside the shore,
Their music to the hills and lonely sands;
But all in vain the memory demands
   A vision of the mute romance of yore.
   We well had said: "It shall return no more.
We beckon back the past with futile hands."

Nay, it was lost till you, with subtlest wiles,
   Recalled the glamor and the mystery —
     The cypress hushed beneath the evening star,
   And haunted headlands graven by the sea —
Till Beauty that was fled from darkness smiles,
   And moonlight is a fane to her afar.

THE MAN I MIGHT HAVE BEEN

Now, ere the grey and ghastly dawn
    Restore the heartening sun,
And Conscience, at his light withdrawn.
    Behold her toil undone,
With more than day's remorseful pow'r,
    To grimmest ghosts akin,
He comes to haunt a candid hour —
    The man I might have been.

Clear-visioned with betraying night,
    I count his merits o'er,
And get no comfort from the sight,
    Nor any cure therefor.
I'd mourn my desecrated years
    (His maimed and sorry twin),
But well he knows my makeshift tears —
    The man I might have been.

Decisively his looks declare
    The heart's divine success;
He held no parley with despair,
    Nor pact with wantonness;
He wanders with accustomed feet
    The heights I dreamt to win;
A sleepless hour, he finds it sweet-
    The man I might have been.

His station in the ranks of good

I view with joyless eyes;
His victories o'er self withstood
    Denying I surmise.
Tho' reason slay him at a glance,
    The mirth of Death agrin
Defines him master of mischance —
    The man I might have been.

Whenas I ponder in my pride
    (An after-dream of day)
If thus the wilful gods deride
    My will to scorn the day,
He comes, where jealous of their youth
    I nurse a starveling sin,
To sting me with the acrid truth —
    The man I might have been.

Tho' half I deem my gentle friends
    Would love him less than me,
No less the daunting wraith attends
    The dark's sincerity.
O Fates that held us at your choice,
    How strange a web ye spin!
Why chose ye not with equal voice
    The man I might have been.

THE TRIUMPH OF BOHEMIA

A WOODLAND MASQUE

(Being the thirtieth annual midsummer High Jinks of
the Bohemian Club of San Francisco, as enacted by
members of the club at the Bohemian Grove in
Sonoma County, California, the twenty-seventh night of
July, Nineteen Hundred and Seven.)

*(The Play is preceded by an orchestral prelude, toward the end of
which the curtain is drawn, disclosing a forest glade at the foot of
a wooded hillside in moonlight. Seven Tree-Spirits are discovered
sleeping. They toss in their slumber and appear perturbed. During
the closing measures of the prelude, the First Tree-Spirit awakes
slowly and half arises.)*

FIRST TREE SPIRIT

(Drowsily)

> Who calls? I fain would sleep. Nay, call me
>   not!
> I cling to sleep! What voices break my rest?

(Rising)

> What power to-night makes heavy all the air,
> And with my slumber mixes dreadful dreams?
> Some spirit stirs malignly! All the dark
> Seems overhung as tho' with monstrous wings,
> And menace loads the gloom. My brothers stir,
> And mutter broken prophecies from sleep.
> 'Tis ominous, nor further to be borne,
> Save in defiance and all watchfulness.

(Touching the other Tree-Spirits)

> O brothers, wake!

(The other Tree-Spirits sleep on, but become more agitated in their slumber.)

Awake! some peril comes!

SECOND TREE-SPIRIT

(Half waking)
Touch not my dream!

FIRST TREE-SPIRIT

(Shaking the sleeping Spirits anxiously)
Awake I A foe is near!

SECOND TREE-SPIRIT

(Rising)
The night is strange! I vow some witch hath
passed
And spat a curse. My dreams were dipt in fear.

FIRST TREE-SPIRIT

And mine!

OTHER TREE-SPIRITS

And mine! And mine!

FIRST TREE-SPIRIT

I deem't were well
We should extend some challenge to the wrath —
Demon or lich or ghost — that walks to-night
Our ancient and immutable domain.

SECOND TREE-SPIRIT

*(Addressing the other Tree-Spirits, who have now
arisen and listen with anxious interest.)*

'T were well indeed I What strength is like our
    strength?
Whose home is like to ours? The leaguing rains
Are but our cup-bearers. The tempest wakes
Our deep, enormous music, and expires.
The furious sun but lends intenser life,
And winter's lance is blunted on our breasts.
The mountains are our brothers, and the sea.
Time is our slave. O brothers! let us cry
Defiance to the powers of earth and air!

FIRST TREE-SPIRIT

That cry the mountains know. That cry has rung
These thousand years along this vale of ours.
The centuries have heard our song, and passed.

CHORUS OF TREE-SPIRITS

Like elder gods that congregate —
Like gods that rule a spacious land,
We, from the morn of time made great,
Like Titans mailed, untroubled stand.
Earth's strong and primal sons are we,
And equal of the ageless sea;
August, we hold an ocean's strength;
Our stalwart lives know not their length,
Tho' ancient thrones and empires pass
Like dews at morning from the grass,
Supreme we face the warring sky —
The unharming ages pass us by

Nor conquer us at all.
Upon the mountain wall
At dawn the sun we greet,
At eventide the stars,
As mighty brotherhoods that meet.
We set the tempest bars,
Tho' loud and long it call,
And barriers to the whirlwind's breast —
We scorn their fury and unrest.
The fire shall smite in vain
The pillars of our hall;
Mankind is but a feeble thing;
Time sunders not our endless reign;
Like giants throned we sing;
Defiance proud we fling —
Tho' thunderbolts from heaven may fall,
Tho' all the winds from heaven may swarm —
To lightning, fire, and storm!

FIRST TREE-SPIRIT

Brothers, your souls are wise, your hearts are
strong —
Too strong to fear this menace of the night,
This formless peril of the traitorous dark.
Tho' such appear, we straight with baffling mirth
Shall drive it hence, with arrowy laughter pierce
Its futile mail. Let happiness be arms,
And merriment our refuge and our shield —
The merriment of leaves that shake for joy,
The merriment of brooks and rippling grass.
Ye Saplings, dance in maddest mockery
Of any hostile power that haunts the night!

SECOND TREE-SPIRIT

Dance! for the winds compel your boughs in
    life!
Dance! for the fallen leaf must dance in death!

*(The Tree-Spirits withdraw from the center of the stage, leaving
eight Saplings, who begin a dance. The dance lasts for several
minutes, but is interrupted by the North-Wind Motive in the
orchestra, followed by the appearance of the Spirit of the North-
Wind.)*

SPIRIT OF THE NORTH-WIND

Who challenges the wind, and sets his breast
Against the tempest? Who shall stand unscathed
Before my fury? Let that one come forth!

SECOND TREE-SPIRIT

O Saplings, dance your merriest, nor heed
These empty thunders!
*(The Saplings gaze in terror at the North-Wind,
and hesitate.)*

FIRST TREE-SPIRIT

                        Fear ye not at all;
But dance like summer dust in summer winds.
*(The Saplings resume their dance, at the end of which the North-
Wind Motive is again heard, and the Spirit of the North-Wind
advances with threatening gestures.)*

SPIRIT OF THE NORTH-WIND

I now with voice of imminent prophecy
Announce your dooms, and bid you bow to Death!

SECOND TREE-SPIRIT

Who then art thou who vauntest? Who art thou,
That mightiest things should stand in awe of
    thee?

SPIRIT OF THE NORTH-WIND

I am the North-Wind. On the frozen seas
I have my home, and thence I sally forth
To scourge the world. All living things, abased,
Fall down before me. My resistless hands
Have sundered limb from limb the hugest oaks.
The pine, with broken back, hath bent to me.
I rush athwart the mountain-peak, and shout
My dreadful challenge to the lands below.

FIRST TREE-SPIRIT

I know thee. I am father of the grove,
And from a sapling have I striven with thee,
Nor fallen.

SPIRIT OF THE NORTH-WIND

       Yet thy doom is come, and come
The doom of all thy brothers. I have sworn
Not any life shall brave me in my wrath.

FIRST TREE-SPIRIT

(*Turning to the other Tree-Spirits.*)
    Brothers, draw near, that so we hold in scorn
    These vauntings and immoderate menaces.
(*The Tree-Spirits group themselves before the Spirit of the North-Wind.*)

SPIRIT OF THE NORTH-WIND

And deem ye then that helpless now I stand,
Or that my war is ended ere begun?
Dream not your perils cease: I, too, O Trees I
Am of a brotherhood. All power is ours.
We lay our hands upon the shaken world
And wrench its walls and sturdiest pinnacles.
We drive all life in terror from our front,
And wrap the sea in winding-sheets of foam.
I have prepared this night my war, and now,
O arrogant and unastounded trees!
Mine allies shall announce their offices,
And tell their strengths, and bid you bow to
    Death. . . .

O come, my dreadful brother of the South!
        *(The South-Wind Motive is heard in the
orchestra and the Spirit of the South-Wind appears.)*

SPIRIT OF THE SOUTH-WIND

O Trees! I am the South-Wind! On my brow
Sit drought and acrid fevers of the air.
Before me walk the brood of fervent heat
And phantom armies of the pestilence.
I shall impel upon your heads this night
All poisons and all languors. Ye shall reel
And find the very earth below your feet
Is sick and leprous.

SECOND TREE-SPIRIT

          Nay, the boastful winds
Were ever noisy. We despise thy words.

SPIRIT OF THE NORTH-WIND

Appear, O loyal brother of the West!
(*The West-Wind Motive is heard in the orchestra, and the Spirit
of the West-Wind appears.*)

SPIRIT OF THE WEST-WIND

My cloudy walls look down upon the sea,
And mine unresting children walk her tides.
I am the West-Wind. I shall leap the wall
The mountains rear, and smite you on the flank.
I, lord of all the sea, shall rend your limbs
Even as I strike to foam the howling wave.

SECOND TREE-SPIRIT

Thunders affright us not, nor any threat
That lacketh deeds behind its braggart breath.

SPIRIT OF THE NORTH-WIND

Appear, O brother of the bitter East!
(*The East-Wind Motive is heard in the orchestra, and the Spirit
of the East-Wind appears.*)

SPIRIT OF THE EAST-WIND

Behold me! I am Master of the East!
The white Sierras are my granite throne —
The pathless desert is my resting place.
The world is but my harp, and from its chords
I lift a dolorous music to the sky.
I, pitiless, shall tread you down, O Trees!

SECOND TREE-SPIRIT

So much of sound, so little of assault
Are food for scorn. A boast is not a blow.
We scorn, O Winds! your furious array.

SPIRIT OF THE NORTH-WIND

Allies are ours of whom ye little reck;
O Father Time, come forward in thy pow'r!
(*The Time Motive is heard in the orchestra, and the Spirit of
Time appears, bearing his scythe.*)

SPIRIT OF TIME

Cities of men and groves august with years
Mine eyes have seen. They are forgotten now.
All beauty and all strength await my hands,
Which smite to dust all beauty and all strength.
1 touch the flower; I touch the butterfly;
I break the sceptres and the swords of kings,
And in my fitting seasons rend their tombs,
And sow their fruitless ashes on the wind.
Minister of eternity am I.

FIRST TREE-SPIRIT

We know thee not, nor bend to thee at all,
Except thou gauge with deeds those pomps of
    breath.

SPIRIT OF THE NORTH-WIND

Then, foolish Trees, one whom ye know too well
Shall war with you. Wherefore do thou appear,
spirit and essential soul of Fire!

(The Fire Motive is heard in the orchestra, and the Spirit of Fire appears high on the hill in a burst of flame. He rushes down the hillside, bearing a flaming torch in the form of a scourge. Flames issue from his helmet, and leap from the earth along his path. He reaches a station above the point where the Spirits of the Winds and Time are gathered.)

SPIRIT OF FIRE

I come, whose hunger never yet had glut!

SPIRIT OF THE NORTH-WIND

Greeting, thou changeless terror that dost walk
By noon-day and by night! Behold thy prey!

SPIRIT OF FIRE

(Coming down to the Spirits of the Winds and Time.)
Madness and furious blood untamable
Do mix in me, till merciless I rage.
Before the vision of astonished men
I rear my flaming throne, and glare thereon,
Waking their tears, that cannot quench mine ire,
Hearing their groans, that soon my laughters
    fierce
Do drown; till, rushing onward from their fields
I grasp all swords of elemental pow'r
And drive my harnessed whirlwinds o'er the
    world —
Resistless tempests quickened by my wrath.
(The orchestra here begins the music introductory to the conflict which follows.)

FIRST TREE-SPIRIT

We still defy all perils and all pow'rs!
Stand, brothers, as of yore, for not alone
Shall any life resist the warring world.

SPIRIT OF THE NORTH-WIND

Ye raging and relentless elements
That hold the heavens! Whose voice the
    thunder is,
Whose lance the thunderbolt, whose wings the
    rain,
Come, dreadful in your cloudy panoplies!
With night and storm confound these stubborn
    trees,
 And hurl them shattered from their eminence I
(*Turning to his allies.*)
    On! On! nor pause till all the trees are doomed,
    And ruinous ashes load the victor winds I
(*The Spirits of the Winds, Time and Fire prepare to advance
upon the Tree-Spirits, and descend from their station; the latter
make ready to repel the assault, armed with branches. The stage
is darkened as they rush upon one another, and the conflict is
represented chiefly by the music, augmented by thunder and
lightning and the howling of the wind. As this comes to a close,
the stage gradually becomes bright, and the Tree-Spirits are seen
grouped in the center, their enemies hewing disappeared. The
music that accompanies the conflict merges into the Victory
Chorus, which the Tree-Spirits sing.*)

VICTORY CHORUS

Ye gods of victory
Look down on earth and see
How fail our haughty foes!
Presumptuous they rose,

And dared to dream that we could fall.
Defiant, stern, and strong,
We met their hostile throng,
And now the night beholds us all!
Unconquered in our battle-hall.
O gods of victory!
Look down on us and we
Shall praise your power, unfailing lords,
And cast from all our forest chords
A music glad and long,
A high and happy song,
That fire and time and winds in vain
Assail our everlasting reign,
Victorious and strong.

FIRST TREE-SPIRIT

We have conquered! we have conquered! All in
    vain
The drunk and noisy vaunting of our foes I
We have withstood their onslaught, nor bowed
    down.
Who now shall strive with us for evermore?
Who now shall share with us our ancient place,
Or dream to stand unhumbled in our sight?
(*The sound of a distant horn is heard from the direction of the
hill. The Tree-Spirits peer up the hillside.*)

SECOND TREE-SPIRIT

What god, with distant clarion from the night,
Betrays his frustrate hunting? All the wood
Is hushed to hear that music on the dark.

(The sound of the horn is again heard, but nearer. The orchestra plays a slow march, and a band of Woodmen appear in the distance on the hillside. They carry broad-axes and torches, and one has a horn slung from his shoulder.)

FIRST TREE-SPIRIT

Lo! who are those that come? What shape of
    man
Assaults our solitudes? Man seemed till now
A feeble thing, a red and harmless brute,
That ran all naked in his daily search
For nut and root and egg, or at the stream
Desired the fish. But these are white, and hold
Each one a gleaming weapon in his hand —
The which I fear, not knowing why I fear.
The crimson fire has no such tooth as that.
*(The Woodmen begin to sing the Care-Song as
they approach, and the Tree-Spirits stealthily with-
draw.)*

CARE-SONG

Thro' the wide world everywhere
Restless mortals flee from Care.
Where they marry, where they work,
There shall Care unsleeping lurk.

Tho' I wander far and wide,
Care, a shadow at my side,
Still shall claim his worship due,
Still shall know me and pursue.

All in vain I seek a spot
Where his face shall haunt me not,

Till beneath the shielding sod
I shall hide from Care the god.
(*The Woodmen finish the Care-Song and gaze curiously about them.*)

FIRST WOODMAN

Here, brothers, shall we labor day by day,
And sleep at restful night, till all this grove
Be fallen. These indeed are mighty trees.
How still the night I tho' not so long ago
It seemed as tho' the wind would never fold
His vast and furious wings. Sleep now till dawn
Awake you. As for me, I shall not sleep,
For I must draw my plans against this wood.
Here, first, I set mine axe.
(*First Woodman drives his axe into the nearest tree. A groan is heard. The orchestra plays a fragment of the North-Wind Motive.*)

SECOND WOODMAN

Brother, didst groan?
Methought I heard a sound most grave, as tho'
Far off, a giant knew his doom, and moaned.

FIRST WOODMAN

The sound thou heardst was but the northern wind,
Sobbing his heart out in some hollow tree,
And since he may draw near, it well would seem
That we have shelter from his cruelties.
Come, let us fell the smallest of this grove
And set its boughs between us and the gale.

(The Woodmen grasp their axes and turn toward a tree, but are arrested by the hooting of an owl. They gaze up the hillside, where an immense owl may be seen flying slowly in a spiral course toward them.)

SECOND WOODMAN

What spirit stirs within the shaken dark?
What sweep and dreadful imminence of wings?

FIRST WOODMAN

I see what seems a dragon of the night —
Some wide-winged bat of hell!

SECOND WOODMAN

I ween a god,
Enraged, has sent some herald of his ire
To beat us hence. Now whither shall we fly?
(The owl finally alights on the lower hillside at the back
of the stage and vanishes. At the point where the owl
disappeared, the Spirit of Bohemia, a naked youth, is
seen. The flight of the owl is accompanied in the
orchestra by the Owl Motive, which changes
to the Bohemian Motive when the Spirit of Bohemia
enters. The Woodmen fall back in astonishment.)

SPIRIT OF BOHEMIA

O men! what would ye in my chosen place?
Know ye each tree around is holy wood?

FIRST WOODMAN

Nay, this we knew not.

SPIRIT OF BOHEMIA

         I, Bohemia,
Within these solemn, everlasting aisles,
Do walk at times, and that my tranquil house
Longer endure, within each pillar high
Have set a guardian spirit . . . .Come ye forth
My forest children.
(*The Tree-Spirits emerge from the forest.*)
       Why this pallid fright
That with unwonted spell constrains each face?
What peril threatens?

THIRD TREE-SPIRIT

(*Sings*)
        O thou mighty one!
Give heed, attend our prayer, and set thy strength
Between us and this doom! Harken our cry,
And sit in judgment as we make appeal!
Justice! O thou arraigner of the wrong!

ARIA

O spirit crowned with grace and pow'r
Be with us in this darkest hour!
The might thy majesty attests
Display to guard our anxious breasts,
Nor suffer that unspared we reel
Before the grey, relentless steel.
For ages we, a stalwart band,
Have cast our shadows o'er the land;
For ages shared the peace that fills
The blue dominion of the hills,
And heard at our unmoving feet
Her changeless tale the brook repeat.

We take no part in Nature's harms,
But ever hold protecting arms
O'er humble things that love our shade;
And now must we too soon be laid
In ruin on the mother earth?
Shall all the powers that blessed our birth
Forsake us in our time of need?
Must we be humbled as the reed?
Shall we no more grow fair and tall,
Where woodland voices rise and fall,
Nor feel upon our brows again
The soft caresses of the rain,
Nor know the blessings of the light
And all the comfort of the night?
Defend us, Spirit strong and bright!

SPIRIT OF BOHEMIA

O trees I love, 't is well indeed I came!
Had I held revel in some distant land,
As is my wont, nor thought me of this grove,
And how beneath its shade no care endures,
These men had ravaged, ere again I found
Its refuge, this my place of peace, and wrought
Great desolation. It is well I came.
O men that plot the ruin of my home,
Now get ye hence accursed from this spot!

FIRST WOODMAN

Be merciful, Bohemia! We all
Are needy men and humble. We thy wrath
Deserve not, nor deserve thy dreadful curse.

SPIRIT OF BOHEMIA

O men! O latest men within this land!
Harken my words: Ye, year by cruel year,
Lay desolate the lordliest groves of earth,
And in great woodland chambers of the gods
Do sacrilege. The living miracle
That Nature, careful for a thousand years,
Did so contrive with wisdom to perform,
Ye in a day undo. Did forests know
What ravage was designed them by your minds,
They in one moan more solemn than the sea's
Would sound their lamentation, and affright
All men and lands. Imagine ye, forsooth,
The patient gods will sit forever calm,
Bearing to see their fairest seats profaned,
And these their altars tumbled from the sky?

SECOND WOODMAN

Men too have need of homes.

SPIRIT OF BOHEMIA

                              Truly, and there,
Housed gentlier than soulless bear or wolf,
Should find both heart and mind made sensitive
To cherish beauty, nor desire to pluck
The field's last flower, nor fell the grove's last
        tree.
Behold! The land is armied with these woods!
Ye may fare onward for uncounted leagues,
To hear them murmuring in dawns to be.
Must ye, like kine in corn, spare not a shaft?
Nor will ye in one valley leave one grove?
Ye are no men, but brutes, and now my curse
Shall scatter you abroad like frightened swine!

FIRST WOODMAN

Nay, great Bohemia, let mercy rule
Thy heart! Henceforth this grove is holy
    ground.
At last we see our sin, and so repent
Our sacrilege, and fain would guard these trees.
Permit that we be children too of thine!

SPIRIT OF BOHEMIA

Since ye find grace, to hold in reverence
This grove, I now pronounce it of my realm
Chief temple, and do make you ministers
Of my good worship.

FIRST WOODMAN

                We would serve thy fane
Forever — thou art gladdest of the gods.

SPIRIT OF BOHEMIA

My worship is a happy one, and hath
Large recompense; and in my temple soon
There shall be gracious spirits that attend
In beauty and in strength. . . . O Fire! come
    forth!
(*A fragment of the Fire Motive is heard in the orchestra, and the
Spirit of Fire appears high on the hillside, in a glow of colored
light. He descends the hillside slowly, still surrounded by a colored
glow, till he reaches the lower hillside at back of stage.*)

SPIRIT OF BOHEMIA

Tell now thy service in the years to be.

SPIRIT OF FIRE

Master, I shall light the ritual
And, splendid-robed, make bright the temple
    aisles.
When these thy priests, with melody and song,
Extol thy name, I, glorious on thy hearth,
Shall gild the revel, and dispel all thoughts
That are of darkness. Wherefore, to this grove
I shall not fare henceforth save at thy beck.
Here not as a destroyer shall I rage,
But parent and preserver of the light.

SPIRIT OF BOHEMIA

Come forth, O Winds! and tell my new-made
    priests
Your service.
(*A fragment of the Wind Motives is heard in the orchestra and
the Spirits of the East, West, South and North Winds come on
in the order named.*)

SPIRIT OF THE NORTH-WIND

          High Bohemia! we are come!
It is our thought that we no more molest
This grove with all our fury. We shall serve
As minstrels, as the lords of woodland harps —
Masters of wildest music. We by day
Shall wander joyous in the maze of boughs,
And cast like golden fruit our mellow notes
Below to these thy priests, until, by night,
We so with tenderest breath upon our chords
Shall unto slumber lure their drowsy souls
That they forget awhile they ever lived,

And toiled, and were a-troubled. At our call
The timid god of sleep shall cease to fear,
Approach unawed, and bless them till the dawn.

SPIRIT OF BOHEMIA

Come forth, O thou portentous soul of Time!
(A fragment of the Time Motive is heard in the
orchestra, and the Spirit of Time appears.)

SPIRIT OF BOHEMIA

O Time, what is thy service at my fane?

SPIRIT OF TIME

I shall be very gentle to thy sons.
If aught they mark of me, 't will be my smile.
Even as the welcome shadow of a cloud
My shade shall fall on them, until at last
Desiring rest, they turn to me for sleep,
Like weary children to their father's home.

SPIRIT OF BOHEMIA

O ministers of beauty and' of peace,
Come hither, then, and greet my worshippers.
(*The Spirits of the Winds, Fire and Time descend from the upper
stage, and gather before the Spirit of Bohemia.*)

(*Addressing Tree-Spirits.*)
Ye have beheld with what concern, this night,
I have arraigned the foemen of your house,
And made of it my temple. Here no more
Shall pride nor strife have power, but brother-

hood,
Joy, and the strength of true humility
Cause here the Golden Age to dawn at last.
O Trees, how greatly shall your ancient calm
Renew the hearts of all my children, breathe
A fragrance on their spirits, and make strong
Those spirits to endure all ills of life!
Years shall go by, and ye, my priests, that meet
My gaze to-night, shall pass, and sons to be,
Heirs to the light and love of future years,
Shall sing where ye have sung. These very trees
Shall fall at last, and younger shafts grow tall
To keep unchanged the beauty of this vale.
So pass they — unto every one his life. . . .
But I, Bohemia, I change not at all,
And in a thousand years my faithful sons,
Shall thank, with grateful laughter at their
    feasts,
You, my first-born, the dear sons of my youth,
Who first of men found beautiful this grove. . .
And now, O latest priests of mine, arise!
And we————

*(A prolonged and terrible laugh is heard issuing from the earth.
The Care Motive is heard in the orchestra, and Mammon
appears from an illuminated cave in the hillside.)*

MAMMON

I, god of gold, within my golden cave,
Have heard grave blasphemy — seditious speech
Inimical to my supreme designs.
Seldom mine ears are fed with words like those,
For I am lord of men, and when I speak
They tremble. Well I see, Bohemia,
How thou hast urged as traitors to my rule

These Woodmen, late my serfs, and glad to
    serve.

SPIRIT OF BOHEMIA

Thou seest not all, O Mammon! These are now
Priests of my woodland fane, and have fore-
    sworn
Thine empire.

MAMMON

        Thou dost lie, Bohemia!
My power is second to no other god's:
Ye Woodmen, late my servants, follow me
Unto my caverns!

FIRST WOODMAN

        Nay, thou god of gold!
Our hearts are pledged to purer days than
    thine —
To fairer service and serener joys.

MAMMON

Then, miserable ones, your bones shall rot
In this far place, for I in punishment
With massy sceptre shall set loose your souls
That so defy me.

SPIRIT OF BOHEMIA

        Those are burly words:
Let 's see what 's father of them!

(Mammon advances threateningly. The Tree-Spirits, the Spirits of the Winds, Fire and Time rally around the Woodmen. Mammon pauses.)

MAMMON

(Laughing.)
Ye have made faithful friends I Wherefore
    my wrath
I shall forego, and that I may regain
Your fealty, I smile on you, and blot
Your treason, and remit all penalty,
And promise you large bounty and delights,
If now unto my worship ye return.

FIRST WOODMAN

Thy pleasures and thy punishments, all these
In our refusal have a common fate.
We do despise thy favors.

MAMMON

           O ye clods!
What know ye of the splendors of my reign —
Ye that till now have known humilities?
Listen: in midnight palaces of mine,
Music shall serve you at the gleaming feast
And Bacchus tempt your lips with all his wines.
The Seven Sins shall bare for you their breasts
And lead you to their chambers. All your toil
Shall end, and pleasure clothe you as a robe.
Ye shall go forth as kings, and know all bliss,
Beholding nations as your servitors.
(As Mammon speaks, the Woodmen draw nearer to him with open mouths and staring eyes.)

FIRST WOODMAN

What surety have we of these promised joys?

MAMMON

What surety? This!
(*Mammon strikes the earth with his sceptre, and the door of the cave from which he entered opens again, disclosing the interior bathed in a golden light. From the cave come four grey-bearded gnomes, bearing heavy bags, from' which they scatter handfuls of gold at the feet of the Woodmen.*)

MAMMON

Take these as tokens of the bliss to be
And hasten with me to my city lights.
(*The Woodmen stand uncertain, and gaze alternately upon Mammon and the Spirit of Bohemia.*)

MAMMON

Imagine now the pleasures that await!
The wild wine singing madly in your veins!
The white, permissive breasts! My splendid
    domes!
And ease unbroken in my marble courts!
That heavy ore shall make my livery light.
And purchase for you each his dearest wish.

SPIRIT OF BOHEMIA

Nay, Mammon! for one thing it cannot buy?

MAMMON

What, then, cannot it buy?

SPIRIT OF BOHEMIA

A happy heart!

FIRST WOODMAN

Is that the secret of thy worship, then,
Bohemia? Is happiness thy gift?

SPIRIT OF BOHEMIA

For lasting happiness we turn our eyes
To one alone, and she surrounds you now —
Great Nature, refuge of the weary heart,
And only balm to breasts that have been bruised!
She hath cool hands for every fevered brow,
And gentlest silence for the troubled soul.
Her counsels are most wise. She healeth well,
Having such ministry as calm and sleep.
She is most faithful. Other friends may fail,
But seek ye her in any quiet place,
And smiling, she will rise and give to you
Her kiss, nor tell you any woeful tale.
Entreat her, and she will deny you not;
Abandon her, and she will not pursue.
By gold ye shall not win her, nor by toil,
Nor ever at her side beholding walk
Save in that old simplicity of heart
Her primal lovers brought. So must ye come
As children, little children that believe,
Nor ever doubt her beauty and her faith,
Nor deem her tenderness can change or die. . .
And I, my forest priests, am kin to her:
More happiness hath any day of mine

Than Mammon holds in heavy-hearted years.
I do not proffer lives of craven ease,
Nor tempt your hearts with vampire luxuries
And scarlet-cinctured sins. The gifts I grant
Are man's high heritage — clean toil and sleep,
Beauty, and all her voices in your souls,
And loving friends, and honorable days.
So choose!

MAMMON

Yea, choose!
(*As Mammon speaks, the gnomes again scatter gold at the feet of
the Woodmen, who stand in momentary uncertainty, then with
unanimous impulse kneel before the Spirit of Bohemia.*)

FIRST WOODMAN

O glad Bohemia,
Be thou the master of our happy hearts!
(*Mammon rushes down the hillside, the gnomes gathering about
him when he reaches the platform.*)

MAMMON

Bohemia! thou well dost know that I
And thou are gods; that these who know my
    reign,
And those that serve thee now within this grove,
Are weak against our godhead, nor have pow'r
In any wise upon us. Thou and I
Alone have power, and thou and I this night
Shall battle for the lordship of this grove.
Come forward then, that so we prove the will
Of greater gods than we, and now decide
Whether these silly men and trees and winds

Shall hold this spot, or whether I, supreme,
Shall smite thee down, and dedicate this vale
To desolation and unchanging dearth.

SPIRIT OF BOHEMIA

Mammon, hold not in scorn my followers,
For they shall see thee die. Nor deem thou they
Abide mine only servants — all glad things
Acknowledge me, all sprites and Bacchic fauns,
That now, unheeded by thy grosser sight,
Do throng this wood, and wait to join my train.

MAMMON

All such are less than we. The combat waits.

SPIRIT OF BOHEMIA

O justice latent at the heart of things,
Decide! Send forth thy vengeful minister
In whatso shape thou wilt. Thou, God, decide!
(*The immense owl that heralded the coming of the Spirit of
Bohemia now sweeps down the hillside. Mammon, hearing the
rush of its wings, turns and dies at its touch, the owl
simultaneously disappearing.*)

SPIRIT OF BOHEMIA

The will of the Inexorable is shown.
Wherefore, ye priests and worshippers of mine,
Approach with me, that I may now reveal
Great Mammon's secret. Draw ye close, and
        gaze
Upon those features.

*(The Spirit of Bohemia, together with the First and Second
Wood-Spirits and First and Second Woodmen, and the Spirits of
Fire, Time and the Winds, mount the lower hillside and gather
about the body of Mammon.)*

See, betraying Death
Hath changed that visage, and proclaims to all
That where high Mammon stood and shook his
    mace,
There, masked in undisclosing gold, stood Care!
But come, O friends, and hale his body hence.
Thou, Fire, shalt have thine utmost will of him,
Till ye, O Winds, make merry with his dust.
*(A march is played by the orchestra, and a procession of
Bohemians in robes of red, white and black descends the hillside
slowly. They carry torches, and a bier covered with a pall. As they
reach the point at which the body of Mammon lies, the march
merges into the Final Chorus, which is sung by the Wood-
Spirits and Woodmen. As this comes to a close the hillside is
brilliantly illuminated, the body of Mammon is placed on the bier
and the procession forms for the Cremation of Care.)*

FINIS.

82848745R00055

Made in the USA
Middletown, DE
06 August 2018